E-NEWSLETTERS
THAT WORK

E-Newsletters That Work

The Small Business Owner's
Guide To Creating, Writing
and Managing An Effective
Electronic Newsletter

Michael J. Katz

To order additional copies of this book, contact:
Xlibris Corporation
1-888-795-4274
www.Xlibris.com
Orders@Xlibris.com
17663

CONTENTS

OVERVIEW

CREATING THE CONTENT

Part I—What Do I Write About?

CREATING THE CONTENT

Part II—How Do I Write?

FORMATTING AND LAYOUT

DELIVERY AND LIST MANAGEMENT

APPENDIX I

Outsourcing

APPENDIX II

E-Newsletter Launch Template and Check List

To Linda, in appreciation of your
support, confidence and love.

FOREWORD

Michael Katz's E-Newsletter was about the 300th email newsletter I'd looked at that year. At the time, I was quasi "editor-in-chief" of the Internet Business Forum's suite of over a dozen business-related email newsletters. Part of my job was writing and managing the ibizNewsletters group of publications.

Every week, for over a year, ibizNewsletters highlighted three email newsletters and analyzed each to draw out lessons for those using email to gain and retain customers, readers and/or website visitors. Back then (2000), it wasn't easy to find good role models. (And it hasn't got much easier since, either.) Here was a medium with huge promise for connecting with customers. Yet few businesses were making good on that promise.

Why?

Blame it on a dearth of expertise and experience—something we sought to address with our own articles. But with so many hype-driven sales messages masquerading as newsletters, it often felt like a lonely furrow to plough.

Then Michael's own publication appeared in my inbox. His clarity, wisdom and objectivity spoke for themselves; "At last," I thought, "someone who really understands the potential of email to engage and enthuse the reader." Recognizing a kindred spirit I whisked off a congratulatory email and highlighted Michael's work in various newsletters and online forums.

In the intervening 24 months, and although we live on different continents, a regular exchange of email has led to an electronic friendship based on a common interest in using email for building relationships. Indeed, this friendship is itself a glowing testament to email's potential in this context.

Building relationships with customers is an excellent way of creating or supporting customer loyalty; managing repeat sales and referrals; and a buffer against fickle economies and eager competitors.

And email newsletters are, in turn, a wonderful tool for initiating and cementing such relationships. They let you connect with the customer at a more personal level and enter a mutually-beneficial exchange based on value; you give them useful or entertaining content, and they give you their hearts, minds and wallets in return.

The "problem", of course, is how to make the most of this potential. How to create and publish an email newsletter that binds, rather than *blinds*, readers to your business? That's the tricky part. While there are a heap of resources that focus on the practicalities of email newsletters, there are few that take a genuine business—and relationship-oriented perspective.

Once again, Michael has come to the rescue with this book. Once again, I find myself poised to send him another congratulatory message.

Here you'll find objective and practical advice to help your business get the greatest benefit from publishing your own email newsletter. And that's why I heartily commend it to you.

Who knows, maybe you'll end up becoming a role model yourself.

Dr. Mark Brownlow

Vienna, Austria
December 2002

Publisher, Email Marketing Reports website
Author, The Keeping The Key Report On How To Give Email Newsletters Impact And Influence.

OVERVIEW

1

Introduction

The secret is out. Electronic Newsletters—or E-Newsletters, or Ezines, they're all the same thing—are the best marketing tool to come along in a long time for a small business.

They're forwardable; they're linkable; they're measurable; they're archivable and they're wonderfully interactive.

They generate leads; they increase sales; they open up a two way dialogue with customers; they position your company as an industry thought leader; and they provide you with an instantaneous means for communicating with the outside world.

They have no variable cost, and once set up, they have almost no fixed cost either.

Terrific stuff.

Unfortunately, this silver lining does have a cloud.

Everybody already knows about them. In the business-to-business world in particular, many of us now receive a dozen or more E-Newsletters each week, forcing us to become aggressive "delete key" users, if only to get through the daily pile of email.

Like a favorite restaurant that's been discovered by the masses, the sudden popularity of the E-Newsletter is the biggest threat to its demise.

Fortunately, you can make E-Newsletter clutter work in your favor.

It's not that your customers and prospects are *tired* of receiving useful, relevant, interesting information that can help them in their business or personal lives. In fact, it's just the opposite.

They're tired of receiving the self promoting, "act now while supplies last," in your face junk that characterizes most of what passes for E-Newsletters today.

The opportunity for your small business is to create an E-Newsletter that's different; an E-Newsletter that stands apart from, and above the crowd:

- An E-Newsletter filled with useful, relevant information.
- An E-Newsletter that's written in a clear, genuine voice; that reflects what it's like to do business with your company.
- An E-Newsletter that grows your business by focusing on solidifying relationships with your clients and prospects over the long term, not on hard sales and quick promotions.

That's what this book is all about.

Anybody can send out an E-Newsletter (when you boil it all down, an E-Newsletter is just an email sent in bulk to a list of people).

The challenge is in creating something that people anticipate, open, read, and pass along enthusiastically.

That's when the magic starts to happen, and that's what this book will show you how to do.

2

What is an E-Newsletter?

In the interest of making sure we're all on the same page from the beginning, bear with me for a few paragraphs while I provide some basic structure and definition regarding E-Newsletters.

An E-Newsletter is basically a glorified email. You write a message, stick it in an email, and send it in bulk to a bunch of people who receive it (as an email) on the other end. That's it.

Yes there are many details, moving parts and things to consider in doing it easily and effectively, but when you boil it all down, an E-Newsletter is an email from you to them.

To dig a bit deeper, there are three pieces to an E-Newsletter, each of which is covered in detail in Chapters B-E of this book. Here they are:

- **Content** (Chapters B and C) What you write and how you write it.
- **Formatting / Layout.** (Chapter D) How the words are organized on the page. Fonts, graphics, sections, links, etc. This chapter covers the set up of the newsletter itself.
- **Delivery / List Management.** (Chapter E) Great content and layout are useless without people to send it to and a "machine" for sending it. This section covers how to add, subtract and manage the names on your subscriber list, as

well as what's involved in getting the newsletter out the door efficiently.

Take these three pieces, mix them together, and you've got an E-Newsletter.

3

Why start an E-Newsletter for your business?

If you already send printed materials out to your contact list—whether as a newsletter or in some other fashion—one of the quickest, most tangible benefits you will see in switching to an electronic format is a savings in printing and mailing costs.

Obvious.

What's not so obvious at the outset, are the other benefits that an E-Newsletter presents. Taken together, these will contribute far more to the success of your business than even the significant expense savings that switching from offline printing to online emailing represents.

Specifically, an E-Newsletter will:

- **Increase Lead Generation And Cross Selling**—An E-Newsletter keeps you top of mind with customers and prospects, and provides an ongoing mechanism for highlighting your full range of products and services.
- **Increase Customer Lifetime Value**—Competitors can buy their way into your market by matching your pricing, matching your products and even matching the look and feel of your company. What they can't buy are your relationships. Every newsletter that you send serves to solidify the connection between your company and your customers.

- **Provide A Low Cost, Instantaneous Channel For Sending Messages**—Your database of email addresses gives you instant access to your customers and prospects. With a variable cost approaching zero, you can send alerts, advisories and messages as frequently as you wish.
- **Position You As A Thought Leader And Innovator**—Your E-Newsletter gives you a voice in the market; a podium from which to articulate your company vision and demonstrate your leadership.
- **Open Up A Two-Way Dialogue With Customers And Prospects**—E-Newsletters allow recipients to easily and immediately interact with you. Comments are made, information is requested, an exchange of ideas between you and your customers flows easily in both directions.
- **Hypercharge Your Existing Marketing Efforts**—Your E-Newsletter doesn't compete with your web site, print newsletter or existing marketing materials; it leverages them. It creates a steady pulse and focus that ties your other marketing efforts together.

Keep these benefits in mind as you launch and develop your E-Newsletter. There's a lot more for you here than *just* saving a few dollars on printing and postage.

4

How much does it cost?

In terms of hard dollars, an E-Newsletter costs practically nothing. One of the great things about going electronic, is that once the format is set up—and assuming you don't pay anybody else to write the content for you—the investment to manage the list and publish the newsletter (i.e. email it to your subscribers) is minimal.

Even when outsourcing to an E-Newsletter vendor (see Appendix I for more detail on outsourcing), it's extremely cheap to keep it running, and for as little as $25 a month, you can create a nicely formatted, professional looking E-Newsletter for your business.

To the extent there's a cost, it comes in the form of time spent. Depending on how many people you involve in the process, how fast you write, and how good you are with detail, **you should figure on about a full day of work per issue** to write it, format it and send it out.

For most people, that breaks out into about 75% getting the words down on paper, and 25% for the remaining logistics.

5

Is it really worth the effort?

Look at all the ways you spend time in the name of marketing your business. Your write articles for professional journals; you take clients and potential clients to lunch; you send holiday cards; you attend trade shows; you ask for referrals; you make cold calls; you attend association meetings.

All of this with the hope of gaining visibility, meeting potential clients, and reinforcing existing relationships. It's a necessary part of running a small business, but if you think about it, it's very much a hit or miss approach.

An E-Newsletter on the other hand, offers all the benefits of these other approaches, but in a much more cost effective and targeted way. **Why wander around business meetings hoping to stumble onto a potential new client, when you've got existing relationships with customers and others that you're not fully nurturing?**

Taking one day per month to connect with your universe of contacts is well worth your time, and in terms of ROI, your E-Newsletter will become the most systematic, most effective marketing activity your small business is engaged in.

6

How do I know if it's working?

There are a number of ways to gauge the contribution and return on investment of your E-Newsletter, some of which will be more obvious and easily measured than others. Taken together, these quantitative and qualitative measures will give you an overall picture of your E-Newsletter's value to your business.

Reduced Expenses.

If you're currently spending hard dollars to market and promote your business (in the form of direct mail, newspaper advertising, sponsorships, printed newsletters, or other "keep our name in front of people" costs), the launch of your E-Newsletter represents an opportunity to cut back on these expenses.

In many cases, the cost of getting your E-Newsletter up and keeping it running can be entirely offset by *not* spending money on other, less productive promotional activities. As a first step, therefore, look for ways that you can use your E-Newsletter to reduce your existing marketing expenses.

Increased Revenue.

Your E-Newsletter will generate leads and sales that are directly attributable to it. For example:

- **Current clients** will contact you to say, "Your last

newsletter made me think of x, and we're wondering what it would cost for us to do something like that."

- **Long time readers** (who you may have never done business with before) will contact you to say, "I've been reading your newsletter for a number of months now, and I like what you've got to say. We have a need for y, can you help us with that?"
- **People you've never heard** of will contact you to say, "A colleague of mine gets your newsletter and forwarded it to me. We've been thinking of doing z, do you do that sort of thing?"

You will have many instances where you can definitively link lead and sales activity to your E-Newsletter.

Stronger Business Relationships.

This last aspect of an E-Newsletter's value, although clearly the hardest to quantify, may in fact have the most far reaching impact for your business.

Because although an E-Newsletter will both reduce your marketing expenses and lead to a measurable increase in sales, its greatest strength is not as a direct marketing tool. **It's most valuable as a relationship building tool.**

If you measure the contribution of your E-Newsletter simply from the perspective of short term, trackable results, you will be missing a lot of what's going on in the background. In order to measure its effectiveness, you need to look much more broadly at the impact it's having on your entire business, and in particular, on your overall relationship with your customers and prospects.

Because you can't easily measure "relationship strength" (much less its ultimate contribution to the bottom line), you will want to track a number of metrics to understand how well your E-Newsletter is doing in this respect. These include:

- The amount of reader feedback received (questions,

comments, suggestions). How many inbound emails are you getting each month?

- The number of new subscribers added each month.
- The number of subscribers who ask to be taken off your list each month.
- The percent of newsletters that are opened each time you publish (see Appendix I, "Outsourcing," for more on how to do this)
- The number of clicks from links you provide within each newsletter (see Appendix I).
- The number of newsletters that are forwarded by your readers to other people each month (see Appendix I).

In gauging the relationship building value of your E-Newsletter, what you're looking for is signs of reader interest. **Interested, engaged people are the ones who bring you their business.**

7

What's likely to go wrong?

Setting aside the time to get your newsletter out the door on a consistent, regular basis is the biggest hurdle you will face in realizing the benefits of an E-Newsletter.

Although it may appear to you at this point that things like deciding what to write about, settling on a format, and figuring out all the ins and outs of the back end logistics, is the hard part, I assure you that as you dig in here and start the ball rolling, all of those details will fall into place.

What I can't guarantee—and the place where most newsletters fail—is your company's ability to motivate itself to do this on a regular, ongoing basis. By month four or five in the life of your E-Newsletter (after the honeymoon period is over), many people feel their initial enthusiasm begin to wane.

Don't let it! Like exercising, you've got to publish regularly and for a period of time, before the benefits start to show up with frequency and clarity.

The good news however, is that like exercise, once you get into a regular schedule, it gets easier and easier to keep it going.

Commit to 12 months at the outset. Give your E-Newsletter a chance to have an impact.

8

The Three Secrets to an Effective E-Newsletter

The rest of this book covers a lot of ground regarding the production of a quality E-Newsletter. Before jumping in with both feet however, I want to call your attention to three BIG concepts that I'd like you to keep in mind as you go about your E-Newsletter business.

I call them "secrets," because as simple as they are, they are completely ignored by 95% of the people and companies producing E-Newsletters today.

Secret #1: Focus on the content

Go to the bookstore and grab a copy of *To Kill a Mockingbird*, by Harper Lee. The 1960 winner of the Pulitzer Prize and one of the top selling books of all time, it's as fresh and engaging as it was 40 years ago.

Now, go to the discount rack and pick up a dusty old loser.

What's the difference between these two books? Why is one so much more successful than the other?

Is it the binding? The cover art? The paper quality? The distribution network that delivered the books to the bookstore? No, no, no and no.

The difference is the content. The text of *To Kill a Mockingbird* scrawled on the back of a restaurant napkin would be a more interesting read than a beautiful, high quality book filled with nothing but blank pages. Content is what matters.

The reason I mention all this is that in the world of E-Newsletters, content is frequently left out of the discussion. Go to E-Newsletter business seminars, read business articles about E-Newsletters, or listen to the E-Newsletter vendors talk about what matters, and content almost never makes it to the top of the list.

The conversations in the E-Newsletter world are overwhelmingly dominated by discussions of tracking, formatting, list management and other logistical aspects of E-Newsletter production.

There's nothing wrong with talking about these things (after all, that's what a good chunk of this book is about), but it's all irrelevant if the content of your E-Newsletter isn't great. **If what you have to say is not interesting, clear, compelling and of use to your readers, then everything else is a waste of time; yours and theirs.**

As you develop your E-Newsletter, remember *To Kill a Mockingbird*. At the end of the day, content is the only differentiator that matters.

Secret #2: Focus on the relationships

The primary reason that E-Newsletters are so powerful, is because they provide a systematic means for growing and maintaining relationships. It's not because they're cheap or trackable or archivable or clickable or forwardable, although they certainly are all those things.

It's because they give you a vehicle for connecting with the people who purchase or are likely to purchase your product or service, month after month after month.

If you write your company newsletter with a focus on enhancing the relationship between you and your readers, you will stand head and shoulders above your competition, most of whom are missing this point entirely, and who (whether they say it out loud or not) view their E-Newsletter as an inexpensive way to send direct mail to their house list.

As you'll see in the following pages, everything we suggest you do in managing your E-Newsletter—from the way you speak to your readers, to the topics you select to write about, to the way you manage requests to be taken off the mailing list—is intended to reinforce your relationship with your customers and prospects.

Secret #3: Be Genuine

A few months ago, I attended a local business meeting where I didn't know anybody. After a few minutes of wandering around, I began talking to a man named Mark, who owned his own executive coaching business. Terrific guy: warm, friendly, smart and easy to talk to.

As it turned out, Mark was just about to launch an E-Newsletter, and upon learning what I did for a living, he asked if I would mind taking a look at it. I said sure, send it over.

What a shock. The newsletter, although filled with useful information and insights, was completely without Mark's personality. It was dry, dull and uncomfortably formal. It was missing the one thing that made Mark stand out in my mind; his vibrant personality.

I sent the newsletter back to Mark suggesting some changes, and in particular, encouraging him to "speak" to his readers in the same genuine way he welcomed me into the meeting the previous week. He did, and what a difference!

Look, many of us were taught to write very formally, and in business writing in particular, we write as if we are appearing in front of a Senate subcommittee on the importance of being serious in the workplace.

Don't do that. Email is an informal, one to one medium, and the stuff that plays well in "The New York Times" reads like dust online. **Be yourself, and give your readers as much of an authentic taste of you in every newsletter as you possibly can.**

CREATING THE CONTENT

Part I—What Do I Write About?

1

What do I write about?

You know a lot more than you may realize.

And although running out of material is one of the biggest fears people have—and one of the primary reasons that companies don't launch E-Newsletters in the first place—**I have never come across anybody who knew enough about a particular industry or topic to start a business in it, who didn't also have a nearly endless supply of content to choose from.**

Remember, your customers and others who have an interest in your area of specialty, don't work in it every day they way you do. The things that are second nature to you, whether it's how to purchase home insurance if you're a broker; how to write a press release if you're a marketing consultant; or how to troubleshoot a light switch if you're an electrician; are all news to those of us on the outside your industry.

These brief, useful nuggets are the things you write about.

The people who are going to read your newsletter have questions. You on the other hand, have answers, opinions, experience, and perspective. When it comes to your industry, you understand what matters and what doesn't, and how all the pieces fit together.

Your challenge in selecting topics therefore, is not having *enough* to write about. It's identifying which things are the most useful, the most interesting and the most relevant.

Here's how you get to that:

Sit down with a blank piece of paper and write down as many *questions* as you can think of regarding your business. Write down the things that your customers, prospective customers, colleagues, friends and relatives ask you every day in relation to your work. When they come to you for an insider's perspective, what is it that they want to know?

"How do I . . . ?"

"Should I . . . ?"

"What do you think about . . . ?"

"How do I know if . . . ?"

"Is it worth spending money on . . . ?

"What would you recommend for . . . ?"

"What will happen if . . . ?"

All these individual nuggets of information that you work with and think about and pore over every day, are the content of your newsletter. Start making your list now!

—*QuickTip*—
What do I write about?

There's nothing worse than having a great idea for a newsletter column while jogging one morning, only to forget what it was entirely when you sit down to write two weeks later.

Keep your list of column ideas in a place you can easily find (I have a Word file on my computer called, "Future Columns"), and every time you think of something interesting for a future issue, put it in there.

Not only does this prevent the "what do I write about" blues, you will be amazed at how quickly the good ideas pile up once you have a place to pile them. When it's time to write each month, you simply open the file, look around for the idea that's most compelling, and off you go.

2

How broad or narrow should my topics be?

Remember that one of the key benefits of an E-Newsletter is that it reinforces your position as an expert in the eyes of the outside world.

With that in mind, your objective is to match the content of your newsletter to the content of your business, so that:

1. You attract readers who are potential customers for whatever product or service you sell.
2. You remain top of mind among these readers, so that when they have a need on this topic they come to you.

Your readers will naturally assume that what you write about is what you do. Match the content of your E-Newsletter to the business you are in, and you will attract buyers of your services.

3

How do I define my target audience?

OK, so you've got the knowledge you need to develop the content.

Knowledge however, is only part of the puzzle. We've all listened to speakers or read articles written by people who were obvious experts in their field, but who were unable to communicate effectively. **There's a big difference between knowing something yourself and being able to explain it to an audience.**

And the biggest barrier to making that happen is being clear on who the audience is. Without a clear definition, you won't know what tone of voice to use, which metaphors make sense, how much detail to provide, or even which topics are the most compelling.

Defining your newsletter audience is critical. Here's the best route I've found to accomplishing this:

Think about a specific person among your customers or contacts who you want to address your E-Newsletter to. Not a demographic group; a real live person that you know. Now think about things like what she does for a living; what her problems are; how much she knows about your industry. **As you write your E-Newsletter each month, write it to her.**

I know that this may seem counterintuitive, since by selecting a single person to write to, we are by definition excluding everybody else. What I've discovered however, is that the natural tendency to write to as broad an audience as possible—in the hope of appealing to a wide variety of people—results in content that is generic and impersonal, the exact opposite of what you're looking for.

To counteract this, you'll want to overcompensate in the other direction by picking a single person to talk to. This in turn leads to focused, genuine, conversational copy; the holy grail of E-Newsletter content.

—*Quick Tip*—
Defining the Audience

You may be in a position where you have more than one potential audience for your E-Newsletter: employees; consumer clients; commercial clients; peers.

The more dissimilar these groups are, the harder it will be for you to deliver content that is useful, relevant and interesting across the board. Keep in mind therefore, that there is a point where you are better off creating more than one newsletter, rather than trying to speak to many groups through a single, one-size-fits-all vehicle.

4

How do I keep from "giving too much away?"

After doing a presentation to a small business organization on the value of E-Newsletters, I was approached by a member of the audience who came up to me with a concerned look on his face.

He identified himself as a plumber, and told me that his fear was that by writing a newsletter filled with plumbing tips he, "would be giving his expertise away."

I assured him that he had nothing to worry about.

First of all, it's a newsletter, not a textbook. We're giving away tips, views, nuggets, insights. Reading 12 (or even 52) of these tips a year isn't going to turn me into a master plumber.

Secondly, even if he were to write a full length book and send it to his customers, he still wouldn't be putting himself out of business. There are already dozens of "how to" plumbing books on bookstore shelves, and if the existence of the information alone were enough to put him out of business, it would have happened long ago.

Two things to keep in mind:

1. There's a big difference between reading a newsletter or book, and having the expert by your side working on your specific problem. One is generic, one size fits all

information. The other is focused,
an experienced professional. No com

2. The more you give away, the more t
reveal, the more your customers will com
the expert in your field. And (ironically) th
they are to hire you to do more work for them
to refer you to their friends and colleagues.

The bottom line is that it is virtually impossible to g
too much away in your newsletter. Help your readers the wa
you would a friend; the rest will take care of itself.

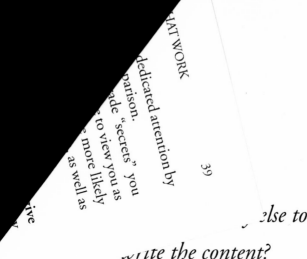

…else to

…write the content?

You can, but I'd encourage you not to.

Remember, as "Secret #2" says, E-Newsletters are all about relationships. Your newsletter should give potential customers a taste of what you're like, who you are, what you believe in, what you know about your industry, and what doing business with you is all about (for existing customers, it's an ongoing reminder of all these things).

If you hire somebody else to come up with topics and write the content, you risk losing this real connection. Now, instead of your newsletter extending your company out to its customers, it simply becomes an information piece. No relationship, no genuine interaction, no "here's what makes us different from all the other firms in the industry."

All that said, having somebody else write or edit the content is manageable, provided you keep a couple of guidelines in mind:

1. **The ideas should be yours**—so that your expertise, perspective and unique point of view come through.
2. **It needs to read like you talking (writing)**—so that your true personality comes through.

Bottom Line: If you hate writing (or just don't have the time), but still want to reap the benefits of an E-Newsletter, go ahead and bring somebody in to work with you. Just make sure that the writer gets the meat of the topic ideas from you, and always give it the once over before it goes out the door to ensure that it reads like you wrote it.

6

Should I survey readers to find out what they want?

An occasional reader survey is a nice way to stir up the conversation between you and your readers. It's inherently interactive, and the results fold back nicely as topics for future issues.

In terms of getting a handle on what people want you to write about however, it tends not to be very effective.

The problem is that the response level to "what do you want to read" surveys is very low, and the answers you get aren't necessarily accurate representations of the interests of your audience as a whole.

The best way to know what people want to hear about is to train yourself to pay attention to what they ask about and talk about during the course of your work every day. The important, burning issues in your industry are already out on the table, you simply need to watch for them and pick them up when you see them.

7

What if I run out of things to write about?

This is a common question, and it stems from an underlying belief that there is a limited supply of good topics out there. If you believe the "Good Topic Well" is going to run dry, it makes sense to pace yourself, and save some of it for some time in the future.

Believe me, this won't happen, and saving topics for the future is a bad idea.

The way to produce a great newsletter, is to publish great stuff, month after month after month. Always take the most important, the most compelling, the most insightful idea you've got at the moment and use it.

Here's why:

1. **Your writing will reflect the urgency that you feel.** The best articles are the ones that reflect your current passion, and if you put a topic on the shelf for some time in the future, it won't feel the same when you come back to it.
2. **You won't run out of the good stuff (really).** In fact, publishing good stuff will lead to more great stuff as readers complement you and you sit back and proudly view what you've put out into the world.

Give the world the best you've got every time you sit down to write, and you'll never go dry.

8

Should I build up a stockpile of articles before I launch?

Whether from concern over running out of content, or concern about not getting around to writing each month, some people try to write a bunch of newsletters ahead of time—before they launch the first issue—in an attempt to have a supply handy in case they need it.

This too is a bad idea.

1. **It delays your launch.** Putting off launching, "until we have two / five / a year's worth," will extend your launch date. The time it takes you to write these to your satisfaction is time you could be out there building relationships, developing your business and improving your newsletter.

2. **The articles won't feel fresh.** Newsletters are primarily a communications tool; a proxy for the face to face interactions that you'd like to have, but can't have with all your customers every day. Prewritten articles sound stale.

    Imagine if you wrote out all the holiday, birthday, and anniversary cards for your spouse, for the entire year, ahead of time. It might be more efficient, but besides not being a real reflection of where you were at that point in time, it would read flat and uninspired.

    Relationships happen in real time, and for your newsletter to be fresh, it needs to be written that way as well.

CREATING THE CONTENT
Part II—How Do I Write?

1

What do I do if I can't write?

I hear it every day from the small business owners I work with: "I can't put out an E-Newsletter, I'm a lousy writer."

Here's the good news: Writing a newsletter is a lot more like talking than writing.

People don't expect to read prose on screen, and they don't want something that reads like an article from a local business journal. They want a piece of you and your expertise.

The most effective E-Newsletters are those that sound as if the company leader is just talking, filled with all the slang, run on sentences and joking around that comes out in person.

Look, relationships happen between people (not between organizations), and the more you can write in a genuine, spoken manner, the more it will feel to readers like somebody (i.e. you) is really on the other end.

So don't worry about your ability to turn out something that your high school English teacher would be proud of. Turn out something that breaks down the walls between your company and your customers and you will be just fine.

2

What's the right mix of promotional Vs. "real" content?

One of the biggest mistakes made by company E-Newsletters, is that the focus is mostly on the company doing the writing. Here's what we have on sale; here's an award that we've just won; here's a seminar we are holding next month; here's one of our employees who just got promoted, etc.

It's important to include this type of information, but you can't lead with it, nor can you let it dominate your E-Newsletter. If you do, you'll turn people off, they'll unsubscribe, and your opportunity for ongoing communication will be reduced.

Here's the rule: 80% of your newsletter should be focused on helping the reader; 20% should be about you.

Don't worry, you're not, "giving away 80% of the real estate" when you do this. Your newsletter is not a radio ad, it's (all together now) . . . a relationship!! Focus on establishing that, and you don't need much space to sell.

You're selling in the most effective way possible when you provide useful information, and only as an aside, mention what else you're working on.

So go ahead, drop in a link to your seminar; mention the award you've just won, tell me about how many charities you support. But do it separate from the main body of the newsletter

(I have a special section devoted to, "Shameless Self Promotion"), and don't do a lot of it.

Remember, 80/20.

—*Quick Tip*—
About Us

Each newsletter should include an "About Us" (or similarly named) section near the end. This brief, one or two line summary of what you do—your "elevator statement"—is an elegant way to talk about yourself without talking about yourself.

Unlike the "Shameless Self Promotion" section mentioned above which highlights recent company accomplishments, the About Us section should be a relatively constant statement about your business (Mine is: Blue Penguin Development, Inc. helps companies increase sales by showing them how to market to their existing relationships).

When the day comes that this summary matches up with an immediate need of a reader, you will get a call.

3

Should I hire an editor?

For a small business, I advise against the hiring of an editor.

An editor is a trained expert in smoothing the bumps, sanding the edges, and organizing thoughts. And although I'm not suggesting that you go out of your way to write in a bumpy, splinter filled, unorganized way, I am saying that if that's the way you talk, act, look and work, then you want all this to shine through. Your newsletter should read as if you are there talking.

All that said, I would recommend that you have somebody else read it through, at least for the first few issues. But not an editor, and preferably not somebody in your industry.

Believe it or not, the best person for this role tends to be a spouse, and if you've got one of those hanging around the house, that's who I would recruit.

Your spouse knows you well enough to determine if your writing sounds like you speaking, and yet in most cases, he/she probably doesn't know as much about your industry as a true insider (and therefore will be sensitive to jargon, or writing that assumes the reader knows too much).

If you don't have a spouse, see if you can find somebody else who knows you well, and whose arm you can twist to help out.

4

How opinionated should I be?

News is a commodity, expert opinions are priceless.

Your newsletter is an opportunity for your company to become a respected voice in your industry; a thought leader. **That requires that you express an opinion, explain a concept, take a stand. It requires that you take a position.**

If all you are is a secondary source of news, and all your newsletter does is rehash and summarize industry events and the thoughts of others, your readers will see that and will soon find their way to the original sources of information.

Taking a position is a lot easier than you might think. You live within your industry every day, and you know what's going on. You know what's working, what's controversial, what's important, and what's just plain stupid. You can't help but have an opinion on what's going on around you.

Your personal point of view is what's most useful to your readers. Remember, they're on the outside looking in, and by giving them your perspective—whether you're an attorney, an electrician, a marketing consultant, whatever—you are saving them lots of time and energy by explaining what's happening.

You don't have to be fanatical or obnoxious about where you stand (although some of the most interesting E-Newsletters are written by people who are), but you do need to have a viewpoint.

Incidentally, there's a very big additional benefit to taking a position. As you confidently state your views each month, you will find—maybe for the first time in the history of your company—that you and your coworkers start to gain a greater understanding and clarity about what you believe in. Writing your thoughts down forces you to focus, which in turn focuses your actions and ultimately, your business.

5

How technical should the
E-Newsletter be?

As lawyer Joe Miller in the movie "Philadelphia," Denzel Washington repeatedly interrupts people in mid-sentence with the request that they, "explain it to me like I'm an 8 year old."

Joe Miller would have made a good E-Newsletter writer.

This is not the place to impress your readers with your extensive vocabulary or to use a metaphor that only somebody with a master's degree in philosophy can relate to.

Even if your subject matter is technical, your writing style should not be, unless you're absolutely sure that all the people reading your E-Newsletter are equally capable.

My friend Bruce Horwitz provides a great example of how to do this well. His monthly E-Newsletter—"TechRoadmap Directions"—focuses on providing patent related information to the legal industry. I don't have a day of law school in my educational background, and I frankly couldn't care less about patents. But I read Bruce's E-Newsletter because it's funny, interesting, and easy to understand, even for a complete outsider like myself.

Keep it simple.

6

Should I copy the experts in my field?

You may be tempted to copy the E-Newsletter approaches of some of the acknowledged gurus in your industry, thinking that if he/she does it this way, that's the way it should be done. Generally, this is a bad idea.

First of all, as we've said before, imitating somebody else never works to your advantage. If all your newsletter does is copy somebody else's style, I may as well read theirs instead of yours.

Second, the gurus are often successful *despite* themselves. Management expert Tom Peters comes to mind for example, as somebody who breaks every rule in the book when he publishes his rambling, ranting, unformatted, unedited, once in a while E-Newsletter.

Tom can get away with it because he is at the point in his career that people are willing to wade through all the communication barriers he inserts, just to get to the gems that he always seems to deliver. For the rest of us, we need to remove the obstacles, not assume that readers will climb over them to get to the good stuff.

Read what the experts have to say, but have the confidence to blaze your own trail.

7

How much hyperlinking is appropriate?

One of the great benefits of an electronic newsletter (and the web in general) is the ease with which anybody can connect pieces of information together. "Hyperlinking" is the act of creating a clickable link from one place (like your E-Newsletter) to another place on the web.

It's easy, it's natural (when you mention a person, company, event, article, etc.), and it requires no prior permission from the place you link to (as long as the place you link to is open and available to anybody surfing the web).

Hyperlinking is what the web is all about!

In terms of how much to hyperlink, think in terms of a lunchtime business conversation, and (as long as we're talking about lunch) "lightly salt" hyperlinks throughout your newsletter.

Just as you would very likely mention relevant people, places and things to a lunchtime companion, use that same approach to creating links.

Keep in mind however, that you're not trying to be an encyclopedia; you're playing the role of the informed expert. Use your knowledge of useful, interesting and relevant resources to round out what you've got to say.

By finding the balance between your own original thoughts and the thoughts of others, you will cement your position as a connected expert who knows the field.

8

Is it a good idea to use stories and metaphors?

People like hearing stories. They're easy to digest and easy to remember, and they add a personal touch to what might otherwise be a dry business discussion.

Where possible, weave stories from your own life into your newsletter.

- Talk about projects you've done with clients.
- Reference personal experiences with your kids, your hobbies or your friends, as lead ins to a bigger concept
- Use metaphors we all understand as a means for clarifying a key point.

Dry facts and intelligent insight by themselves are not enough to make your E-Newsletter engaging. Readers need a hook and real world point of reference to easily assimilate what you've got to say, and a story that they can understand and remember goes a long way in getting your point across.

9

Should I mention my clients in my newsletter?

If you can work (positive!) client experiences into your newsletter, everybody benefits.

- Your client benefits because her business is given exposure to your audience.
- You benefit because you get to demonstrate that you know what you're talking about (i.e. you help real people solve real problems), and that you're somebody who takes care of his clients (i.e. gets them publicity).

Your reader benefits because client stories provide tangible examples of problems solved, and are excellent tools for showing the reader what he can do to improve his own circumstances.

—*QuickTip*—
Using Client Names

Get permission before ever using a client's name.

In fact, to be especially careful not to damage a client relationship in any way, I typically write the newsletter text and share it with my client before publication, to make sure that every word of what I intend to say is pre-approved.

10

Why is reader feedback so important?

One of the most useful aspects of sending a newsletter electronically is the ability of readers to easily and instantly send their thoughts back upstream to you. Not even "The New York Times" or the "The Wall Street Journal" can match your ability to immediately know what your readers are thinking.

This feedback is extremely valuable for two reasons:

1. **The information is useful.** The arrival of your E-Newsletter into the mailbox of your customers will often remind them of some aspect of doing business with you, and prompt a comment. Suddenly, customers who never would have bothered to pick up the phone or send a letter, won't think anything of shooting off a quick email to complain, compliment or question something about your business.

    Engaging these commenting customers in a dialogue is tremendously valuable in both improving your relationship with that particular person, as well as in using these comments to improve the way you run your business.

2. **Reader feedback reduces reader turnover.** Feedback from readers can (and should) be cycled back into future newsletters. Not only do the writers enjoy seeing their words and name in print, but it shows other readers that there are other people out there reading what they're

reading. This helps to create a sense of community and membership, and is very powerful in stemming unsubscribes to your E-Newsletter.

—*QuickTip*—
Reader Feedback

Most people who send you comments will be thrilled to have those comments and their name appear in a feedback section of a future newsletter. But always make sure you first get permission.

Simply send an email back thanking the reader, and ask if you can use what they said in a future issue.

11

How do I get readers to give me feedback?

OK, so feedback is a good thing. But how do you make it happen?

- **The most effective means for getting readers to speak up, is to showcase feedback from other readers.** When I see that other readers are making comments, and that these comments are welcomed (and in fact, celebrated) by the company that writes the newsletter, I am much more likely to send my thoughts as well.
- **The second way it to explicitly ask for feedback at every turn.** Most people need a lot of prompting to get them to speak up, and your job is to prompt them. That means that in every newsletter you send there should be within it a, "click here to tell us what you think," or similarly worded link.

    Also, when you make a point on a particularly interesting or controversial topic, invite your readers to speak back, by saying something like: "Do you agree? Click here to tell us what you think!"
- **Finally, make it easy for your readers to send comments.** Make sure you've got it set up so that by simply clicking "reply," I can respond as I would to any other email.

Don't force a reader—as some E-Newsletters do—to type in some other address to "send feedback," or to go to a web site to fill in a "feedback form." These seemingly minor additional steps will *drastically* reduce the amount of input you get from readers.

FORMATTING AND LAYOUT

1

How important is it to send an HTML (graphical) newsletter?

Content is the key to an effective E-Newsletter, and without that, all the pretty pictures, cool layouts and impressive design in the world won't help you.

However, assuming you've got your content where it ought to be, and given how easy and inexpensive its become to create an HTML newsletter (see Appendix I), you are putting yourself at a disadvantage by not doing this:

- Studies have shown that HTML email has a much higher read rate and click through rate than plain text.
- An HTML E-Newsletter that resembles your web site, includes your logo, and has the freedom to use bold, italic and other visual tools for emphasizing points, looks more professional and is easier to read.
- HTML newsletters provide useful tracking data such as open rates and click rates. Text newsletters do not have this capability, and you forgo a great deal of insight regarding what's going on behind the scenes if you send a text only newsletter.
- An HTML E-Newsletter requires more upfront effort than its plain text counterpart, and therefore implies to your readers that there's some commitment on your part to putting this out on a regular basis.

Taken together, it makes sense to go HTML. This isn't an absolute must have for launch, but I would head in this direction as soon as you can.

—*QuickTip*—
HTML

There's so much you can do with an HTML newsletter, that it's easy to get distracted and forget about the need for well written content. To combat this, write your newsletter each month as a plain word document, without any concern for how it will ultimately look, and completely independent of whatever HTML template you use.

This way, you'll be separating what you've got to say from the way it looks, ensuring that when the final package comes together, you'll have both the steak and the sizzle covered.

2

How do I manage HTML Vs. AOL Vs. text versions of my newsletter?

In the print world, a newsletter publisher has complete control over the look and feel of the final product. Typeface, font size, format, paper quality, graphics, are all chosen by the *sender*, and the final product is exactly the same for everyone, regardless of who it's sent to.

Not so in the electronic world. Here, the recipient's particular computer system and setup comes into play as well, and just because you send your newsletter in a certain way (in HTML format for example), it doesn't mean that everybody who gets it, will see it the same way.

In the old days (like 24 months ago), you therefore had to either send HTML to everyone (knowing full well that some readers had setups that couldn't read it), or you had to bring everything down to the lowest common denominator (i.e. plain text), or you had to keep more than one set of lists, and send different versions to different people.

I'm happy to say that those pathetic days are over. Any capable outsourcer that you use (see Appendix I), will as part of their standard service, create several different versions of your newsletter to make sure it's readable by any and all of your recipients:

- **An HTML version.** This is the preferred version. It looks like a web page, and can have graphics, stylized text, and images.

- **A text version.** For those readers who either don't want, or can't view HTML with their particular set up. These people will see just text—not fancy, but readable.
- **An AOL version.** AOL's email system is proprietary, and depending on the particular version, can see some things but not others. Your vendor will pull out all the people with AOL addresses (which may very well be 50% of your readers), and send them a specially formatted AOL edition.

What's great about all this is that you write and create just one version, and your vendor sorts your list of readers and makes sure that the appropriate version ends up in the right hands. This one aspect alone is a very compelling reason for outsourcing newsletter delivery.

3

Can I just send the newsletter as an email attachment?

A workaround to the formatting dilemma discussed in the previous section is to send the newsletter as an attachment, usually as a Word document or a PDF file.

There are a number of very good reasons for *not* doing this:

1. **It only works if the recipient has the same software as the software you use to create the file (e.g. Word, Acrobat).** Otherwise, they won't be able to open the newsletter.
2. **Viruses come as attachments.** Many people (myself included) will not open email attachments from people they don't know well. Since many people on your list will fall into this category, you will have a large negative impact on your open rate if you go this route.
3. **It introduces an additional step.** Our goal is to maximize the number of people who open the newsletter when we send it. An attachment requires the recipient to not just open the email, but to click on the attachment and wait for it to open as well. Every additional barrier that you put in the way will reduce readership, and this is a significant one.
4. **Attachments can be big files.** I received a 2 megabyte (that's very big) E-Newsletter as an attachment the other

day, resulting in a 5 minute delay while that monster made its way into my email box. By the time it got there I was so mad that I just deleted it.

4

What's the best editorial format?

This question comes up a lot, and the answer is . . .
. . . there is no best editorial format.

I've seen excellent E-Newsletters with a main article and a few tidbits; I've seen excellent E-Newsletters that have a single, simple thought and nothing more; and I've seen excellent E-Newsletters that have several small snippets on a given theme.

There is no one size fits all winning formula for E-Newsletter layout, and provided you follow the other guidelines discussed in this book, you have a lot of freedom to develop a format that feels right to you.

One thing the best ones do have in common however, is that they make a single, clear point. Whether one article or several, there's a central theme with each issue, and the reader walks away having learned something that he or she can easily remember.

Every time you sit down to write your E-Newsletter therefore, make sure you are clear on what this single point is (hint: if you can't write a clear, catchy headline, you probably haven't yet isolated that single point).

5

How long should my newsletter be?

If you could write an effective E-Newsletter with just one word, that would be perfect. Shorter is better. Since that's not so easy to do, shoot for 500-700 words.

Here's why;

- It's hard to read on a computer screen. Study after study has been done and they all reach the same conclusion: nobody likes it. If your E-Newsletter is too long, people will bail out, or worse yet, unsubscribe.
- If your E-Newsletters are long—regardless of how good they are—your readers will learn this after a while, and will tend to, "save this for when I have a few spare minutes." Unfortunately, in the lives of busy people this translates into saving this (unopened) until approximately forever.

At 500-700 words, you've got plenty of space to make a good strong point, without fear that you'll be moved to the "someday" pile.

6

How important is the newsletter name?

Naming your E-Newsletter may seem like a trivial piece of non-business fluff. It's not; it's all a part of creating something that people will read and remember.

Lots of companies don't bother titling their newsletters at all, or if they do, they name it something mind-numbing like, "Community Bank's Monthly Newsletter."

Yawn. Imagine if Stephen King called his next book, *Book #8 by Stephen King*. Somehow, calling it *Misery* is a lot more compelling.

The purpose of a title is to create a brand, a buzz, a theme for what your E-Newsletter is all about. It's intended to give your readers (and prospective readers) a sense of its contents.

Don't be shy here, come up with something catchy and clever that people will think about, tell their friends about, and remember. Small business marketing is largely about standing out from the crowd, and your E-Newsletter title is a key piece to making that happen.

In addition to the main title, your E-Newsletter should have a subheading.

My newsletter for example, is called, "Michael Katz's E-Newsletter on E-Newsletters," with the subheading, "E-Newsletter Insights For A Changing Economy." The first time you see that, you have a pretty good idea of whether or not you want to keep reading. It tells what the benefit is and what it's all about.

A good subheading helps in a couple of ways:

- **It reminds people what they've subscribed to.** In the barrage of emails that your readers receive on a daily basis, some of them may forget from month to month who you are and what you write about, or even that they opted in to receive your E-Newsletter in the first place. Every time they open it they need to be reoriented about what this thing is.
- **It helps new readers.** When one of your subscribers forwards your newsletter on to a friend—one of the main benefits of writing in the electronic world in the first place—a good descriptive subheading will serve to properly orient the new reader, who very likely has never even heard of you.

7

Should I sign the newsletter?

Absolutely. Remember, this is a letter, not a newspaper article. For maximum relationship building power, every newsletter should have your name, title and contact information in it.

The approach I like best is to "hand deliver" the newsletter.

Similar to scribbling a message on a sticky note and attaching it to an article that you might send to a colleague or client, include a brief, opening statement with each issue.

Say hello, mention something topical (the weather, how bad the Red Sox are, whatever), give a quick overview of what this issue is all about, and sign your name as you would any other business letter.

You've got a lot of freedom to connect here—much more so than in a printed newspaper or magazine—and the last thing you want to do is copy the stodgy, impersonal set up of most printed publications.

Remind your readers that there are human beings behind the company walls—sign your name and say hello!

—*QuickTip*—
Sign Your Name

You don't need to include an actual image of your signature here (although if you can get that to work, that's terrific).

Simply including your full name and title accomplishes what we're talking about in this section.

8

Should I "force" a visit to my web site?

There are two schools of thought regarding how to send E-Newsletter content to readers, each with its own set of pros and cons.

School #1: Some people send only article *summaries* in the newsletter itself, and include hyperlinks back to the company web site for those who want to read the full articles.

School #2: Some people include the *entire text* of the articles in the newsletter.

The advantage of the first approach is that it gets the reader back to the company web site, increasing the likelihood that they'll see something, buy something or do something in addition to reading the newsletter. It also introduces an addition layer of measurability, since the clicks to the individual articles can be counted.

The downside of #1 however, is that it requires an extra step for the reader (who must go to the web site), and makes reading offline (as many AOL users like to do) impossible.

I'm in favor of #2. First, because I want to make the experience as convenient as possible for my readers. Second, because I want my E-Newsletter to be read, and the less barriers I put in the way, the more likely this is to occur.

9

Should I sell ads in my newsletter?

Selling ad space in popular E-Newsletters is quite common today. Advertisers realize that subscribers who have voluntarily agreed to receive information on a particular topic are much more likely to open and read one of these emails than email that arrives from an unexpected stranger.

From the perspective of a potential advertiser therefore, it makes a lot of sense to buy space in one of these E-Newsletters. And from your perspective as the E-Newsletter owner, this may seem like an efficient way to generate some incremental revenue.

The problem is that advertising is a distraction to your readers, and has the potential to compromise your entire relationship with them.

A "perfect" E-Newsletter is a conversation between friends, resulting in the building of trust and the ongoing purchasing and referral of your product or service. Just as you would never invite a bunch of friends over to your house and then surprise them by bringing in a salesman to talk about his product, you lose a lot more than you gain when you allow other people to drop their ads into your E-Newsletter.

Advertising is fine, but not in the middle of a relationship.

10

What's an "opt-out message" and what should it say?

At the bottom of each newsletter that you send, it's considered good form to show people how to get *off* the list. Not doing so sends the message that they are captive (whether this is an intentional message or not).

You always want to put your reader at ease and in control. So make sure you include text that says something to the effect of:

> *"You're getting this because you requested it, you're a customer, you're a member of our organization (whatever), and if you don't want to get it anymore, simply (insert instructions for how to get off the list)."*

That's all you need to do.

Taking the opposite approach of making it hard or inconvenient for readers to leave, in the hope that they'll stick around longer, doesn't help your cause. You will lose many more readers with this strategy than by simply inviting them to go whenever they want.

11

What's a "forward to a friend" message and what should it say?

One of the best litmus tests of a quality E-Newsletter is that your current readers are forwarding it and recommending it to other people. When people you've never heard of start requesting that they be added to the list, you'll know this is starting to happen (congratulations!).

To help the process along, you'll want to explicitly encourage forwarding within the newsletter itself. Depending on the web sophistication of your readers, many may not realize it's OK—or even possible—to simply forward it on.

Here's a sample of the forward to a friend text that I use:

> *"Spread the word! If you enjoy reading this newsletter, and have a friend or colleague who you believe might also benefit from it, please forward it on. Anyone can sign up for a free, privacy-protected subscription by clicking here."*

A few things to note about the paragraph above:

1. I explicitly ask people to forward the newsletter along.
2. I make it clear that anybody can sign up.
3. I make it clear that it's privacy protected.
4. I tell them how to sign up, in this case, by "clicking here."

—*Quick Tip*—
Forward to a Friend

Interestingly, putting the words "Please Forward" in parenthesis at the end of each issue's subject line has also—surprisingly enough—been shown to increase the likelihood of a pass along.

12

What's the benefit of archiving past newsletters on my web site?

Once you've got four or five E-Newsletters under your belt, you'll want to begin archiving these on your web site (you could do it right from the start, but it frankly looks a bit odd to have an archive with one newsletter in it).

There are a few reasons why archiving is a good idea, all of which highlight the advantages of electronic newsletters over their print cousins:

1. You'll find that as you write each newsletter, it's natural to reference things you've said in previous issues (e.g. "A few months ago we spoke about the importance of blah, blah."). This is an opportunity to create a hyperlink back to the previous issue, giving the reader more information if they want, without your having to retell a concept or story. Since you'll be adding new readers constantly, the archive allows new readers the opportunity to see things you've already written.

2. An archive gives people a chance to check you out, since your body of work will be a reflection of your expertise, your approach to business and your company personality. This allows prospective readers to decide if they want to subscribe, and prospective clients a chance to get to know you.

3. An emailed newsletter vanishes the minute it's sent. If it's archived, it's there and available until you decide otherwise.

4. An archive naturally draws people back to your web site, increasing the likelihood that they'll interact with other parts of the site and with you.

5. Archived newsletters will be found by search engines. As people out on the web search for information, some of them will be pointed to your archived newsletters. If they like what they see, many will "climb back up" to the top page of your site to take a closer look at your company.

13

Are there particular page layout considerations to keep in mind?

Not only don't people like to read on a computer screen, they often don't read at all—they scan.

To help them get through your material as easily as possible, you'll want to incorporate some simple formatting techniques:

- Use a lot of bulleted lists.
- Break the text up into short paragraphs (two or three sentences), even though it may not "technically" be time for a new paragraph.
- Be aware that readers who are viewing your newsletter as a text file will see "typewriter" formatting only. That means no bold, no italic, and uniform text size. The only formatting they will see are things which appear on your keyboard, such as * * *, ####### and =====. For text readers, using these keys to break up sections cleanly will greatly increase readability.
- Stay away from underlines entirely as a means of emphasis. In the online world underlines have come to be equated with "clickability," and it only confuses the reader who may try and click on an underlined word that you were merely giving emphasis to.

14

Should I number and date the E-Newsletter?

There are some things from the offline world of print publications that are worth copying. One of these is numbering and dating.

Every issue of every legitimate printed magazine or newspaper includes information about:

- **Volume**—indicating which year of publication we're in (first, second, etc.)
- **Number**—indicating which issue in a particular volume this is.
- **Date**—month and year of publication.

The primary purpose of this in the context of your E-Newsletter is to demonstrate that you are committed to publishing on a regular basis, and that this E-Newsletter is an integral part of what you do.

If your E-Newsletter feels like a random collection of thoughts that are kicked out whenever the spirit moves you, you are less likely to develop a following of interested readers. By dating and numbering it however, your newsletter feels systematic and regular.

In addition, once you've produced your E-Newsletter for a while, the mere fact that you are several issues into it will help to establish in the minds of potential subscribers that you have been at this for a while, and are in fact an expert in your field.

15

Do I need a copyright notice?

As soon as you write something, it's copyrighted. You own it, and nobody can use your words without your permission. You don't need to do anything more.

Putting the words, "Copyright © 2003, Blue Penguin Development, Inc," on your publication however, accomplishes a couple of additional things:

- It warns people not to steal your thoughts. The Internet still has a frontier mentality, and people who would never steal things in the offline world sometimes forget themselves and take and reuse content without permission. A copyright notice reminds them not to.
- A copyright notice says, "this is valuable information, and I'm an expert." It reinforces the significance of what you're doing in the minds of your readers, who assume that, "if it's copyrighted, it must be valuable."

—QuickTip—
Copyright Notice

This tip is a bit tricky, so watch closely.

Although you want to protect your rights to what you've written, you still want people to redistribute your E-Newsletter as broadly as possible, provided they credit you as the source.

Your objective therefore, is to let readers know the work is copyrighted, but to give them permission at the same time to share it.
Here's the copyright notice I use:

Copyright © 2003 Blue Penguin Development, Inc. All rights reserved (but feel free to copy it, post it, quote it, think about it and forward on to others).

16

Other recommendations for formatting your E-Newsletter

1. **Include a synopsis at the very beginning**

   Not every subscriber will want to read every issue you send out (I'm sorry to have to be the one to tell you this). It doesn't mean they don't want to continue receiving your E-Newsletter, it just means that for whatever reason, this topic on this day is not important enough for them to take the time.

   To help readers quickly decide if the topic of the month is useful, include a brief synopsis—an executive summary— at the beginning of each column. Something that indicates what they'll find. This way, busy readers can read on if it's relevant, but quickly delete if it's not.

   Your readers will appreciate your respect for their time, and the fact that you are allowing them to control their experience.

2. **Include a privacy notice at sign up and in every issue.**

   There's a heightened concern for privacy on the Internet, and given how much spam we all receive every day, people are naturally wary of giving their email address out to just anybody.

   Put your reader's mind at ease by including a few sentences at the bottom of each newsletter and at the time of sign up, indicating your respect for their privacy. It doesn't have to be complicated, just clear. For example:

"Blue Penguin Development respects your privacy. We do not sell, rent or share your information with anybody, and will only use this data to send you the information you have requested."

3. **Provide an alternative means of contacting you**

Even though your E-Newsletter subscribers expect to hear from you via email, there may be times where they want to contact you some other way. Their subscription may not be working correctly, their computer may be broken, they may be in the middle of switching to a new Internet service provider, whatever.

By giving subscribers an "out of band" means for contacting you (phone number and snail mail address), they can reach you when there's a problem with the medium of choice.

Include your offline contact information on your web site and in each E-Newsletter.

DELIVERY
AND LIST
MANAGEMENT

1

Who do I send the newsletter to?

Your E-Newsletter mailing list begins with your list of existing relationships.
This may be just a handful of friends, family and colleagues if you're just starting out in business, or it may be several thousand customers and prospects from your house list if you've been up and running for some time.

Either way, the fundamental point is that you start with the people you know, and build from there. "People you know" is a very broad definition, but *only includes those who have already had some interaction with you or your company.*

As tempting as it may be to send your E-Newsletter out to every email address that you can get your hands on (by buying addresses, hiring telemarketers to query companies, raiding association lists, etc.), not only will you be wasting your time, you may even be doing damage to your company's reputation in the process.

Remember that one of the primary reasons E-Newsletters are so much more effective than unsolicited email is because E-Newsletters put you in front of people whom you already know (or who have specifically asked to hear from you). **The further you move down the continuum from blood relative to complete stranger, the more watered down your newsletter's impact becomes, and at some point you are simply sending junk email.**

Yes quantity matters—the more people who read and value your E-Newsletter, the more likely they are to bring business your way; either their own, or that of their colleagues.

But all newsletter subscribers are not created equal, and quantity for its own sake is of no value to you. People who delete your newsletter the minute it arrives each month, or (even worse) who are annoyed that you've sent them an unsolicited, unwanted piece of junk email (and who make a mental note to that effect regarding doing business with you in the future), don't help your cause, even if they help raise your subscriber count.

Stop focusing so much energy on finding new people to talk to, and work from the "inside out," by starting with the people you already know.

2

How do people subscribe and unsubscribe?

In terms of how you manage the list itself, remember that conceptually, an E-Newsletter is identical to sending a bulk email out to a group, and the process of E-Newsletter "list management" is nothing more than adding and deleting names from a big list.

Whatever you do, keep in mind that your primary objective is to make it as obvious and easy as possible for people to get on and off your list.

Manual Approach

If you are manually managing your list of names, the simplest approach is to take whatever email system you currently use (e.g. Outlook, Eudora, AOL, etc.), and establish an "E-Newsletter Group" within it.

This is simply a bulk address that you set up with all your subscriber addresses in it, so that when it's time to publish your newsletter each month, you send it once to the group instead of over and over again to each individual.

In terms of how a subscriber gets on your list, keep it simple: On your web site and in the E-Newsletter itself, give people an address to send their request to ("To be added or removed from this list, simply send an email with your request to . . . ")

You get the emails as they come in and make the change. Easy.

Sooner or later however, your list will grow to a size where handling each request just takes too much time. Certainly by the time you get 100 names, I strongly recommend that you subscribe to an outsourcing service to streamline this duty (see Appendix I).

Automated Approach

Even the most basic E-Newsletter outsourcing service will offer some type of system for streamlining the process of adding and deleting names. This is typically done in one of two ways:

1. Subscribers send an email to a specific email address with a request to "subscribe" or "unsubscribe." The emails come in and are *automatically* added or deleted from your list.
2. Subscribers go to your web site, insert their email address into a designated text box, and click a button to get on and off the list. Here too, the adding and deleting is done automatically, without any need for your intervention.

Whichever of these two approaches is used, your vendor will provide you with directions on how to set it up. It's simple to do, and removes you from the administrative loop of managing your list of names.

3

How much subscriber information should I require at sign-up?

You need just one piece of information to send somebody your E-Newsletter: their email address.

I understand that you might be *interested* in knowing their name, occupation, location, household income and blood type, but you don't *need* any of this, and making it a condition of entry will scare some people away.

It's hard enough getting someone to express an interest in receiving another piece of email, and when they finally do come to you with a request, the last thing you want to do is put an obstruction in the way.

It's fine to request additional information, but only require the email address itself.

4

How often should I publish?

Without a doubt, this is one of the top three most frequently asked E-Newsletter questions. I've come to learn that what people are really asking is, "What's the *least* often I can publish and still have it be effective?"

The answer is, monthly. Anything less frequent, and you may as well not bother. Here's why:

1. **Less than monthly isn't often enough to establish a relationship.** You need to appear regularly for readers to get to know you, get a sense of what you do for clients, and keep you top of mind as a company to call on when they have a need you might be able to fill.
2. **The less often you publish, the more likely your readers are to forget who you are in the first place.** As that begins to happen, readers begin to delete without opening and ultimately unsubscribe.
3. **The more often you write, the *easier* it gets.** Really. Monthly gives you the freedom to put a single, simple thought out there, knowing that you'll be up to bat again in just 30 days. If you write less frequently than that, your newsletter will instead feel like a project, and you'll agonize and sweat over it each time.

By the way, in case you're considering publishing *more* often than monthly, I would recommend against that as well. Getting this out the door is hard enough, and you can always tighten the schedule up later if you find that you're getting great results and you love doing it. But don't set yourself up for failure by being overly ambitious out of the gate.

5

Is there a particular day of week / time of day that's most effective?

The conventional wisdom is that mid-day, mid-week is the best time to catch people's attention. It's past the craziness of Monday morning, and not yet into the weekend where (supposedly) nobody is paying attention anymore.

Personally, while I agree that staying away from Monday is a good idea (with two days of emails stacked up, people are very quick to hit the delete button), I highly recommend publishing on a Friday.

People seem to be looking for a bit of a diversion by Friday, and a short piece of wisdom at that point is often very well received.

—QuickTip—
What's the best day of the week to publish?

Don't forget to consider your own writing schedule in choosing a publication date. Another reason I like Friday is that I can "see it coming" at the beginning of the week.

I once managed an E-Newsletter that came out every Monday morning, and even after a year of doing it, it always snuck up on me. I spent many an unhappy Sunday night getting it out the door!

6

Do I need to publish on the same day each month?

Set a publication schedule and stick with it. First Tuesday of the month; last Friday of the month; 15ᵗʰ of the month, whatever.

Believe it or not, this is less for the benefit of your readers than for you (many devoted readers can't tell you what day of the month or even how frequently a particular newsletter comes out).

Having a firm schedule eliminates the feeling that your next newsletter is always hanging over your head waiting to be written. When it's regularly scheduled, it just becomes a regular part of your work and the mental pain of continually putting it off goes away.

Honest.

7

What are "bouncebacks" and what do I do with them?

Depending on the make up of your audience, as many as 5% of the emails that you send out each month will "bounce back" to you. "Bouncebacks" refers to the emails that come back with some kind of error message as "undeliverable."

These typically result from:

- **Dead addresses**—people move, leave jobs, etc.
- **Vacation messages**—"I will be away from the office until . . ."
- **Full mailboxes**—your recipients' Internet service provider allots each account a certain amount of mailbox space, and if they don't check it periodically, it fills up and new emails are bounced back to the sender.

Having these bad addresses on your list isn't a problem in and of itself, and has no negative impact on your ability to send your E-Newsletter to the valid addresses.

That said, it's good practice to delete these bad names periodically. Not only is it annoying to have the same names keep bouncing back to you, if you use an outsourcer it may cost you more, since outsourcer pricing is primarily a function of list size (bad addresses and all).

In terms of which to get rid of and which to keep . . .

• If it's simply a vacation message, just leave it alone. They'll be back.

• If it's a "mailbox full" or a "recipient not found," or a "permanent fatal error," it's a pretty good indication that your subscriber has moved on. In the interest of not removing anybody who may still be out there however, I recommend waiting until an email address bounces back three times before taking it off. At that point, you can be pretty sure that your words are no longer being read.

Many of the email vendors will automatically categorize and sort these for you, grouping them based on why they bounced back. Short of that, you'll need to open up the individual bounce back messages and read what it says about why a particular message wasn't delivered.

8

What goes in the "from" field when I send the newsletter?

According to a study by emarketer, 77% of emails from unknown sources are deleted without ever being opened.

To prevent your newsletter from being accidentally deleted as spam therefore, you need to make it very clear that it's from a trusted, requested source.

So, if your *company name* is most well known to readers, make sure that the "from" field in the email is the company name.

If you *personally* are most well known to readers, use your name.

Don't use the name of the E-Newsletter itself, since that is sure to be the least familiar with readers and more likely to trigger a delete.

9

What goes in the "subject" line when I send the newsletter?

The "from" field of the E-Newsletter tells me it's from you. But why should I bother to open it? The email subject line is your opportunity to pique my interest.

Just as newspapers use catchy headlines to get you to read the articles, your subject heading is another factor that stands between "open" and "delete."

I get many E-Newsletters that simply state the name of the newsletter (e.g. Marketing Newsletter, November, 2002). Although that may alert me to the fact that it's not spam, it still doesn't compel me to open it and read it.

To keep the deletes at bay, do your best to think up a brief, catchy title for each article, and include this in the subject line. **Give me a reason to open your E-Newsletter.**

10

What's a "welcome message" and what should it say?

OK, I've decided to subscribe to your E-Newsletter. I've seen a few issues; I've checked out your web site; I like what you've got to say and how you say it.

So I fill in the form on your web site and hit the "submit" button to sign up. What happens next? In the case of many E-Newsletters, nothing.

Effective E-Newsletters don't let this happen; they welcome new subscribers with open arms.

In practice, this means that as soon as somebody signs up for your newsletter, they should receive a confirmation email (a "welcome message") from you *within the next 24 hours.*

This welcome is important for two reasons:

1. It reassures the reader that their subscription was received successfully (remember, if they happen to sign up the day *after* your last newsletter was published, it might be another 30 days before they get the next one).
2. It welcomes them into your "home" with a warm, friendly message.

A welcome message should include:

*   A thank you to the subscriber for joining.

- A brief statement with a reminder of what the newsletter is about, and an indication of when it will arrive each month.
- An invitation to send feedback, thoughts, comments, etc., to you at any time.
- A signature (name, title, contact information) of a real live person within your organization at the bottom.

The welcome message is the first thing that a new subscriber receives from you. Don't pass up the opportunity to reach out your hand and greet a new friend.

11

What's a "goodbye message" and what should it say?

Several years ago I was hiring for a position, and had two candidates vying for the job. It was close, and either person could have done it, but after some careful thought I choose Julie, and made a job offer.

Once she accepted, I called the other candidate, Mark, told him the bad news, and wished him well. **Not only did he thank me for my time over the previous few weeks, he even sent me a written thank you note a few days later.**

Two weeks later—one day before her start date—Julie backed out of the job to say she had accepted something else. Guess who I ran and hired that same afternoon.

Sometimes, it's the way you handle rejection that tells the most about you. When somebody decides to opt out of your E-Newsletter therefore, take advantage of the opportunity to say good-bye *gracefully*.

Send them an email—also within 24 hours—thanking them for having subscribed and wishing them well.

—QuickTip—
Good-bye Messages

Don't forget to include a request for feedback in your good-bye message.

Not only does this demonstrate a degree of professionalism on your part, it will also unearth some very useful insights, since past subscribers tend to be more frank about what they don't like than current subscribers.

Use this feedback to improve your newsletter.

12

Is it OK to rent my list of names to noncompeting companies.?

Depending on the size of your subscriber list and the narrowness of your niche, you may be approached by other companies wishing to rent or buy your address list.

Please don't do this.

Your newsletter list is an asset that will take you months and months of hard work to build. It represents a relationship between your company and a group of people who have an interest in what you've got to say, and who have given you permission to talk to them each month. Selling (or renting) this hard earned trust is, in a word, insane.

The fact is, your relationship with your readers may be one of the few truly defendable, competition-proof assets that your business has. Competitors can buy their way into your market by matching your pricing, matching your products and even matching the look and feel of your company. What they can't buy are your relationships.

Every name on your E-Newsletter list represents a barrier to a competitor who can do nothing to quickly compete with the strength of your contacts.

Treat these names like the gold they are; don't share them.

FINAL THOUGHTS

By now I'm sure it's clear to you that there are many details involved in getting an E-Newsletter just right. I hope this book has succeeded in giving you a useful framework and valuable guidance for pulling all that together.

I want to leave you with one final thought on the subject of E-Newsletters, and it's a thought that many people have found useful in keeping their newsletter on track:

Host your own party.

When I'm asked to sum up how best to think about a small company E-Newsletter, the metaphor I use is that of a party, with you as the host.

Your job is to set the atmosphere; welcome people when they arrive; introduce the guests to each other; make sure the conversation is interesting and lively; help everyone have a good time; and thank people when they leave. And (perhaps most importantly), you need to make sure that the focus of the event is on the guests, rather than on you.

If you can create something that has the feel of a terrific party, you will be on track to building strong relationships with your customers and prospects, and to building a business that continues to grow and prosper for many years to come.

Thank you again for purchasing, *E-Newsletters That Work.*
Please feel free to contact me with your thoughts and comments
at any time.

Best wishes for success in all you do,

Michael J. Katz
Founder and Chief Penguin
Blue Penguin Development, Inc.
Hopkinton, MA
508-478-6258 mk@BluePenguinDevelopment.com

APPENDIX I

Outsourcing

OUTSOURCING

Throughout this book we have talked about "outsourcers." Whether we call them outsourcers, third party vendors, ASPs, or something else, they all do more or less the same thing: These companies provide a self service (typically web based) means for automating various aspects of your E-Newsletter.

For a very low set up fee and monthly service charge, outsourcers have simplified and eliminated many of the hurdles which used to be in the way of a nontechnical, small business owner developing an attractive, easily managed E-Newsletter.

The cost/benefit ratio has gotten so low in fact, that there is simply no point anymore in *not* outsourcing at least some portion of your E-Newsletter to a vendor.

1

What parts should I outsource to a vendor?

Until very recently (within the last year or two), a small business owner had just two options in developing an E-Newsletter.

You either had to pay a designer/web developer to take care of the whole thing each month, or you had to be content with sending a plain text message out, and using some kind of home grown, jerry rigged back end to manage the list and do the mailing.

Happily, all that has changed. Today, there are over a dozen vendors offering E-Newsletter services, and there are many good, simple solutions at reasonable prices.

The particulars of the different service offerings vary, but overall, these are the kinds of things that can and should be outsourced:

- **Formatting and Layout.** Includes template customization (from simple cut and paste to custom designed solutions); an easy means for creating an HTML (graphical) email; automatic sorting and reformatting of the newsletter into plain text and AOL versions.
- **Delivery.** Includes prescheduled drop date and option of immediate delivery of emails.
- **List Management.** Includes automation of the subscribe / unsubscribe process; sending of welcome and good-bye

messages; importing and exporting of addresses into a secure location on the vendor server; bounceback management.

- **Tracking.** Includes subscriber sorts and real time counts; tracking of emails opened; tracking of links clicked; tracking of emails forwarded to friends; other statistics.

2

What parts should I not outsource to a vendor?

I'm hoping you've already guessed the answer to this: The Content!

As we've talked about throughout this book, the content is the true differentiator and value add of an E-Newsletter, and although I believe you should hand off the mechanical, grunt work of list management as soon as possible, when it comes to content development, I highly recommend that you do this yourself.

The bottom line is that you will have a difficult time creating an E-Newsletter that truly differentiates you from your competition, if your content doesn't look, feel, smell and taste like a genuine part of your company.

3

How much does it cost?

For as little as $15 per thousand emails sent (pricing schemes vary, but start in this range), you get all the things mentioned earlier (some vendors charge a small set up fee as well).

This means that if you send out a monthly newsletter to 2000 subscribers, your cost would be around $30 a month.

To put this into perspective, that same $30 would have only bought you about half an hour of a web developer or designer's time in the days when there were no other options.

4

Is there a risk in outsourcing?

There are two risks to consider in outsourcing. The first is extremely unlikely; the second although more likely, is easily handled.

- **Risk #1: Privacy and Security.** When you use a third party to manage your list, you will be putting your customer list in the hands of that company. In the unlikely event that the security or privacy of that company is compromised, your list could be as well.

  I say unlikely event, because security and privacy of customer lists is of the highest priority to any reputable E-Newsletter vendor, and other than storing the names for you, you don't have to worry that they will contact your customers directly, try to sell the names to a third party, or anything like that.

  All that said, any time you hand somebody your customer list, you do introduce an element of risk, and you should be aware that it exists.

- **Risk #2: Losing the List.** The subscriber emails that you collect over time are a valuable asset to you. Suppose you log onto your vendor web site one day, and it's been shut down. Your E-Newsletter is also shut down if you don't have a back up copy of the list.

  Which is why, to manage this risk, you need to back up your subscriber list regularly (at least weekly). This is an easy procedure (make sure this feature is offered by any vendor you choose), and simply involves downloading the list from your account on the vendor site to a local computer.

This way, if the vendor goes belly up, you simply sign on with another provider, upload your list, and you're up and running again.

5

How do I choose a vendor?

As you can imagine, the answer to this question could be a book all by itself. There are many service variations to choose from, and it's very much a moving target as new players come and go, and pricing and features change.

Even so, there are some fundamental things to look for as you compare service offerings:

- **Tech Support.** Free, live tech support is offered by some, but not all outsourcers. Personally, I wouldn't go near a vendor that didn't offer this.

  Hopefully, you won't need help very often, but when you're sitting at your desk unable to figure out why you can't fix a simple problem, you want somebody to call. Not email support either. A toll free phone number that you can dial during (at least) normal business hours, and within minutes be speaking to a real person.

- **Longevity.** As we mentioned in the previous section, the cost to you of your vendor going under is pretty small. But it's still a whole lot better if it doesn't happen.

  If they fold, you'll need to change horses, which at the very least will require that you learn a new system for getting your newsletter out the door. Plus, a company that is about to die will usually fade slowly, which means they'll stop investing in new features and may even foul up some of your mailings before being declared legally dead.

Before you sign up, go to vendor web sites and read about them. How long has it been since they've introduced new features; have they recently gotten outside funding; how many customers do they have? Look for signs of life and prosperity.

- **Ease of Use.** If you're reading this book, odds are that you personally are the one responsible for getting the newsletter out the door each month. I'm also willing to bet that you're a businessperson, not a techy.

  If both of these are true, you want to make sure that whichever vendor you go with provides you with a platform that requires minimum effort, minimum training and minimum technical knowledge.

  In comparing options therefore, pay a lot of attention to what it takes to set it up, and what it takes to publish it each month. I love features, flexibility, tracking, etc., but first and foremost I need a simple tool that I can use.

- **Free Trial.** Service quality and ease of use are tough to assess from the outside looking in. And as much as you may talk to colleagues and compare options on paper, nothing is as enlightening as actually getting behind the wheel and taking the service for a spin.

  Look for a vendor that will let you sign up for free with no obligation for a period of time (like 30 days). That will give you time to try it out (even if it's with just a few names), see how easy the service is to use, and get a sense for how well the whole thing hangs together.

APPENDIX II

E-Newsletter
Launch Template
and
Check List

E-NEWSLETTER LAUNCH TEMPLATE AND CHECK LIST

The purpose of this template is to systematically guide you through the thought process of developing your E-Newsletter. When you've answered all the questions, and put all the pieces in place, you will be ready to launch.

Important Note: Complete this *after* you've gone through the book!

Content Development

1. **What makes you different?** What's unique about you, your company, your services, etc.? *Beyond* the usual quality, service, price stuff. What are you known for and what aspects of you and the way you do business will you bring out in your newsletter?

2. **Who's your target audience?** Who's the target given your purpose? Clearly there are many possibilities, but if you had to define the quintessential person, what does he/she look like? Age, sex, job title, years of experience, type of business, etc.

3. **What will you write about?** Do a brain dump. Make a list of every topic you can think of related to your business. In particular, look for those things that will be of most interest and use to your target audience as you've described them.

4. **Newsletter Voice and Personality.** Who is "talking?" What is this person's background? How would readers describe him/her?

E-Newsletter Format

1. The name of the newsletter is:

2. The subheading of the newsletter is:

3. The sign up invitation included in every newsletter is:

4. The opt-out message included in every newsletter is:

5. The forward to a friend message included in every newsletter is:

6. The privacy policy included in every newsletter is:

7. The "About Us" section of the newsletter says:

8. In every newsletter, make sure you include:
____ An edition number and date
____ Complete company contact information
____ An overview of this month's content
____ A copyright notice
____ An introductory note

E-Newsletter Delivery and List Management

1. The newsletter will be sent "from":

2. If a reader clicks "reply," their response will go to (email address):

3. The newsletter will be published _____ (Monthly? Weekly?), on the following day: _____

4. People will add themselves to the mailing list by doing the following (going to a web site and filling in a form; sending an email to a specific address; etc.):

5. New subscribers will receive the following welcome message (via email):

6. Subscribers will receive the following good-bye message (via email) when they cancel their subscription:

7. The mailing list will be backed up once a _____ (week, month).
This will be done by: _____ (person's name).

NOTES

NOTES

NOTES

NOTES

ABOUT THE AUTHOR

E-Newsletters That Work author Michael J. Katz is Founder and Chief Penguin of Hopkinton, Massachusetts, Blue Penguin Development, Inc. (BluePenguinDevelopment.com), and is a recognized expert in the creation and management of effective E-Newsletters.

Michael has 20 years of marketing and training experience, and has been directly responsible for the development of E-Newsletters which today boast a combined monthly circulation of over 500,000 subscribers.

In addition to his own bimonthly E-Newsletter—"Michael Katz's E-Newsletter on E-Newsletters"—Michael has written articles for numerous online and print publications, including 1to1 Magazine, Inc.com, CRMguru.com, SearchCRM and WorkZ.

He has a BA from McGill University in Montreal and an MBA from Boston University, and is an adjunct faculty member of the Commonwealth Corporation's Entrepreneurial Training Program.

Contact Michael at: mk@BluePenguinDevelopment.com

Printed in the United States
1243600001B/316-318